SCIENCE FICTION TO SCIENCE FACT

INVISIBILITY CLOAKS

BY HOLLY DUHIG

Gareth Stevens
PUBLISHING

Please visit our website, **www.garethstevens.com.**
For a free color catalog of all our high-quality books,
call toll free 1-800-542-2595 or fax 1-877-542-2596.

Cataloging-in-Publication Data
Names: Duhig, Holly.
Title: Invisibility cloaks / Holly Duhig.
Description: New York : Gareth Stevens Publishing, 2018. |
    Series: Science fiction to science fact | Includes index.
Identifiers: ISBN 9781538214954 (pbk.) | ISBN 9781538213841
    (library bound) | ISBN 9781538214961 (6 pack)
Subjects: LCSH: Optical engineering--Juvenile literature. | Optical
    materials--Juvenile literature. | Camouflage (Military science)
    --Juvenile literature.
Classification: LCC TA1520.D84 2018 | DDC 621.36--dc23

Published in 2018 by
Gareth Stevens Publishing
111 East 14th Street, Suite 349
New York, NY 10003

Written by: Holly Duhig
Edited by: John Wood
Designed by: Matt Rumbelow

Photo credits: This book references J. K. Rowling's Harry Potter
and J. R. R. Tolkien's Lord of the Rings film series for editorial
purposes. These are distributed by Warner Bros. Pictures and
New Line Cinema, respectively. Photo credits: Abbreviations:
l-left, r-right, b-bottom, t-top, c-center, m-middle. All images
courtesy of Shutterstock. With thanks to Getty Images, Thinkstock
Photo and iStockphoto. 2 – Heywide. 5t – Issa_tan. 6tr – Unico_
Anello. 6bl – markara. 7t – DM7. 7b – hin255. 8b – agsandrew.
9t – SFIO CRACHO. 9b – Lukas Gojda. 10t – kasezo. 11t –
chanafoto. 11b – Pecold. 12bl – Somchai Som. 12br – takayuki.
13 – Rinelle. 13inset – severija. 14 – Christopher MacDonald. 15t
– Getmilitaryphotos. 15b – Przemek Tokar. 16 – Kuttelvaserova
Stuchelova. 18 – Alberto Loyo. 19bg – loskutnikov. 19 – Richard
Peterson. 20 – VisionDive. 21 – exkluzive. 22 – Inna Tarnavska.
23bg – Maurizio De Mattei. 23 – Julenochek. 24c – Dizdnk. 25t
– photka. 25bt – megastocker. 25b – kaisorn. 26t – Cheberkus.
26b – Feel good studio. 27bl – Patryk Kosmider. 27b – Rawpixel.
com. 28 – Fresnel. 29 – Viorel Sima. 30t – mdbphoto. 30b –
Stanislav Chegleev.

Printed in China
CPSIA compliance information: Batch CW18GS: For further information
contact Gareth Stevens, New York, New York at 1-800-542-2595.

CONTENTS

Words that appear like this can be found in the glossary on page 31.

INVISIBILITY CLOAKS: THE FANTASY

At one point or another, we have all wished we owned an invisibility cloak. Accidently tripped over in front of your whole school, or called your teacher "Mom"? No problem! Just slip away under your cloak of invisibility. You'd never have to worry about getting dressed again. Who cares what you wear when you're invisible?

Being invisible could get you out of all sorts of trouble, so it's no wonder that it has been one of humankind's greatest desires for hundreds of years. Tales of the legendary King Arthur say that he owned a magical invisibility cloak. It was known as the Mantle of Arthur in Cornwall. The cloak was said to make the wearer invisible while still allowing them to see and hear everything around them.

Of course, nowadays, when people think of invisibility cloaks the first thing that pops into their minds is Harry Potter. We can't hear the words "invisibility cloak" without picturing that bespectacled, scar-headed wizard disappearing under his cloak. Harry's invisible adventures ranged from sneaking into the restricted section of Hogwarts' library to breaking into Gringotts Wizarding Bank. His cloak got him into – and out of – a lot of trouble!

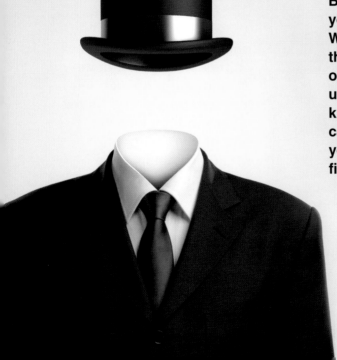

But what would you use your invisibility cloak for? Would you be able to resist the temptation to rob the occasional bank or sneak up on your enemies, if you knew that you wouldn't get caught? Or would you use your powers for good to fight crime and save lives?

In the world of fantasy and science fiction, it is not just cloaks that can make you invisible, but rings too. Possibly the most famous ring of invisibility is the One Ring in J. R. R. Tolkien's Lord of the Rings trilogy. Tolkien warned of the dangers of such a powerful object. In his stories, those who have the ring can be driven mad by its power.

If only one person held the key to invisibility, it might be easy for them to become too powerful, but what would happen if everyone was able to become invisible?

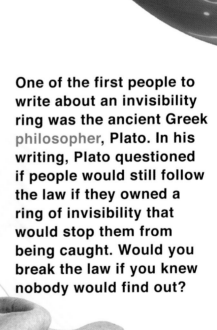

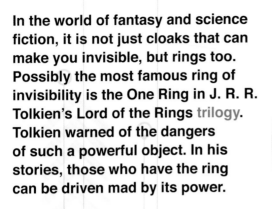

One of the first people to write about an invisibility ring was the ancient Greek philosopher, Plato. In his writing, Plato questioned if people would still follow the law if they owned a ring of invisibility that would stop them from being caught. Would you break the law if you knew nobody would find out?

WHAT DOES THE FUTURE HOLD?

In some science fiction stories, humans are able to fly invisible spaceships. This could come in very handy. Imagine being able to spy on dangerous alien planets without being spotted. Right now, the ability to fly invisible spacecraft and disappear under cloaks belongs firmly in the world of science fiction. But what if scientists could invent invisibility cloaks for everyone? What could we use them for in our earthbound lives? Who knows? We might be picking up invisibility cloaks in our local mall before we know it!

Putting our dreams of invisible space travel aside, how would we use invisibility cloaks if they could be invented now? Well, many scientists are excited about how invisibility cloaks could be used in hospitals by surgeons. They could use them to hide certain parts of the body so they could get a clearer view of the body part they were operating on. One thing's for sure – if invisibility cloaks go from being science fiction to science fact, the world will be a very different place.

BLIND SPOTS: THE SCIENCE OF SIGHT

So how exactly are scientists planning to turn this object of fantasy into a reality?

Before we can look at how to make things invisible, we need to find out how things are visible in the first place! Your eyes use light to see. When light enters your eye, it hits your retina. The retina is a layer of tissue at the back of your eye that is covered in cells called rod cells and cone cells. These cells convert the light that hits your eye into electrical signals, which travel from the retina to your brain via the optic nerve.

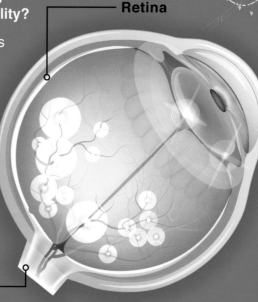

Retina

Optic Nerve

Your eyes collect the information and pass it to the brain, so it can understand what you see. Where the optic nerve connects to your retina there are no rods or cones to collect the light. This creates a blind spot in your vision.

Taking advantage of this blind spot in our vision gives us our first possibility for making things invisible.

EXPERIMENT

Most of the time, you don't notice this blind spot because it is very small and your brain fills in the missing part of the image with what it thinks is there. However, it is possible to become aware of your blind spot. Why not try it yourself?

●   +

Hold this book about an arm's length away from you at eye level.

Then close your right eye and look at the plus sign with your left eye. Keep your left eye on the plus sign as you bring the page closer to your face.

If you keep your eye still, you will notice that the dot becomes briefly invisible, then visible again.

Now repeat the process looking at the dot with your right eye and see if the plus sign disappears!

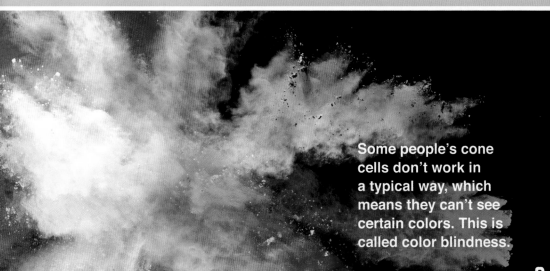

Some people's cone cells don't work in a typical way, which means they can't see certain colors. This is called color blindness.

LIGHT WAVES: COLORS OF THE RAINBOW

Many attempts at creating real-life invisibility cloaks have focused on bending light around an object so we can't see it. But to understand how this could be the beginnings of invisibility cloak technology, we must first understand how light allows us to see, and how we can manipulate it to stop seeing.

PRISM ———————o

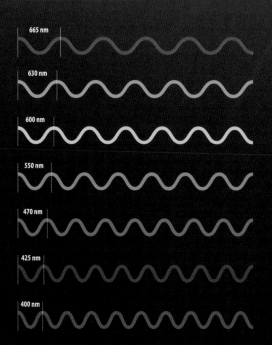

LIGHT WAVES ARE MEASURED IN NANOMETERS.

665 nm

630 nm

600 nm

550 nm

470 nm

425 nm

400 nm

White light – which is the light we get from the Sun and from most light bulbs – travels in a direct path, but is made up of lots of waves. Each wave in white light is a different color depending on its wavelength. A wavelength is the distance between the same point on two waves, whether it be light waves, sound waves, or waves in the ocean. Light is made up of a spectrum of colors, each with different wavelengths. The color with the longest wavelength is red, and the color with the shortest wavelength is violet.

BENDING THE LIGHT

The important thing to know about light is that it can be reflected or refracted. Reflection is when all the light that hits an object bounces off it in the same direction. Refraction is another word for bending. Things that can refract light include certain mirrors, camera lenses, and even heat.

Almost all objects can reflect light. The color of an object depends on which of the wavelengths in light it reflects and which ones it absorbs. For example, a red apple appears red because the apple is able to absorb all the wavelengths in white light except for the long, red ones. These long waves are reflected off the apple, giving it its red color. If we can stop light reflecting off an object by bending the light around it, we could be one step closer to making things invisible!

INVISIBILITY CLOAKS: THE REALITY

Scientists are attempting to design a material that can bend light away from objects. If such a material was created, we could place it over objects to make them invisible. These materials are called metamaterials. Metamaterials are engineered by scientists to have weird and unnatural abilities. Metamaterials may have an important role to play in the science of invisibility cloaks!

In one attempt to make an invisible metamaterial, scientists designed a cloak that, just like the wizard boy's, has lots of complex patterns and details. This might seem pointless. After all, it doesn't matter how fashionable your cloak is when it's going to be invisible! However, the patterns on this metamaterial are not just for decoration. They are designed to be the same length as the light waves that hit them, which allows the cloak to refract the light.

The cloak's material is made from a metal called copper and polycarbonate – a type of material found in the lenses of reading glasses. Unfortunately for us, this cloak is still very much a work in progress, and we might be waiting a long time for it to leave the lab!

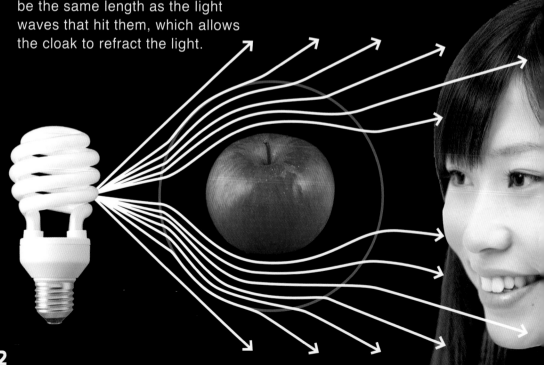

To truly unlock the power of invisibility, scientists need to make a material that can control what colors it reflects. Luckily, in recent years, scientists have moved one step closer to achieving this. They have designed a material made from nano-needles, which should be able to guide light around an object. Nano-needles are far smaller than normal needles, at only 10 nanometers wide. That's 10,000 times smaller than a human hair!

If the nano-needles can bend light around an object, then that object cannot be seen. Once completed, the material would arrange the nano-needles in a cylinder, to guide light around an object placed inside it. The problem is, this cloak only works on red light, and it would need to be able to work on all colors of light to make an object invisible. Perhaps it would work if we paint ourselves red!

NANO-NEEDLES MATERIAL

CAMOUFLAGE: HIDING IN PLAIN SIGHT

CAMOUFLAGE

Camouflage is used to hide an object by making it blend into its surroundings. Many people think that flawless camouflage could be the secret to perfecting invisibility. Some animals have such a good natural camouflage that they can become almost completely invisible in their habitats.

The eastern screech owl is one particularly sneaky master of disguise. Their brown and white feathers look so much like tree bark that they can roost in trees while remaining completely undetected by predators. They also use their disguise to hunt for prey without being seen.

CAN YOU SPOT THE OWL IN THIS PICTURE?

SYSTEM PROTECTION

HOW WE USE CAMOUFLAGE

In the military, soldiers already use camouflage by wearing uniforms with the Universal Camouflage Pattern. Like the feathers on the eastern screech owl, this pattern allows the soldiers to blend into woodland. Other versions of the pattern are designed to help soldiers blend into deserts and urban settings.

However, this type of camouflage is not active camouflage. This means that it doesn't camouflage the soldiers wherever they go – it only does so in certain places. A soldier's uniform cannot change color or blend into any background, and although the uniforms are carefully tested, they do not use any special camouflaging technology.

DESERT CAMOUFLAGE

WOODLAND CAMOUFLAGE

ACTIVE CAMOUFLAGE

COLOR-CHANGING CAMOUFLAGE

While owls use their natural colors to blend into their surroundings, other animals, such as chameleons, are actually able to change the color of their skin.

Chameleons have layers of colored skin under a layer of **transparent** skin. When a chameleon feels an emotion, such as anger or fear, chemicals in their blood tell their skin to display a certain color. For example, when chameleons are angry, they produce chemicals in their blood that turn their skin yellow.

CHAMELEONS CHANGE COLOR TO COMMUNICATE TO EACH OTHER, NOT FOR CAMOUFLAGE. HOWEVER, IF HUMANS DEVELOPED A MATERIAL WITH THE SAME ABILITIES AS A CHAMELEON'S SKIN, IT COULD PAVE THE WAY FOR NEW CAMOUFLAGE TECHNOLOGY.

ΛDΛPTIVE CΛMOUFLΛGE

What if we could become like our multicolored friends and invent a cloak that changed color as we move along? Well, this sort of camouflage technology has already been explored and is surprisingly simple.

Camouflage that can change to blend in with new backgrounds is called active camouflage. In some forms of active camouflage a person wears a jacket made of a highly reflective material while a camera records the scene behind them. The recorded footage is then projected onto the front of the jacket. Another camera records what is happening in front of the wearer, and projects it onto the back of the jacket. This jacket is a neat gadget, but the human eye is not so easily fooled! Our eyes can still detect the outline of the wearer, so we realize that what we are seeing is camera footage.

TRICKS OF THE LIGHT
LIGHT REFRACTION

Sometimes the refraction of light can make us see things that aren't there. If this is possible, then surely we can manipulate light so that we can't see things that *are* there?

Have you ever thought you've seen water running across the road on a hot day? Or heard the classic tale of the thirsty traveler who thinks he sees an **oasis** in the desert, only for it to disappear when he gets too close? These **illusions** are called mirages and they trick us into thinking we can see water that is not there.

Remember, refracted light is just light that is bent. Our eyes use light to create an image of things, so when light is refracted it can make things appear in an unusual way. Heat can often refract light. When a section of air becomes very hot, the light that moves into it from cold air is refracted. In the case of the thirsty traveler, the hot desert air causes light to be refracted, making the ground look like water.

THE MIRAGE CLOAK

Luckily for us, scientists have found a way to use the mirage effect in invisibility cloak technology! They have been able to design a material made from tiny tubes of extremely thin sheets of carbon.

When this material is placed on an object underwater, the tubes heat up the water around it. This means that light rays traveling towards the object are suddenly bent away from it.

This effect works best in water because water is better at refracting light, but that's not very practical for those of us who want to use our invisibility cloaks on dry land. On the other hand, an underwater invisibility cloak would at least keep you hidden from sharks!

However, this is not the only fabric option for future invisibility cloaks. Scientists are also working on a material that combines silk with **microscopic** gold spirals called "split ring resonators" (SRRs) that can refract wavelengths of light around an object.

An invisibility cloak made from silk and laced with gold? Sounds glamorous, right? Well, unfortunately for us, this material cannot yet bend light waves. It is only able to affect other types of waves on the **electromagnetic spectrum**.

Scientists hope that if they can fine-tune this material, it could be used not only to cloak the outside of a person, but the inside too! Because the human body doesn't react badly to silk, this material could be used by a surgeon during an operation.

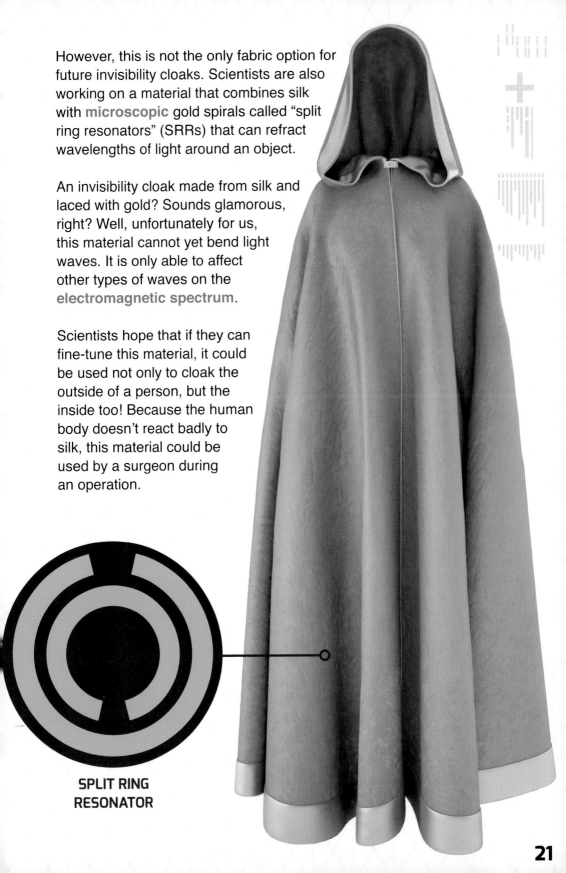

SPLIT RING RESONATOR

INVISIBILITY RINGS: HOLES IN OUR VISION

HOLE IN THE HAND

What if we could make things invisible by tricking the eyes rather than bending the light? Well, technically, we already can! Try this optical illusion at home yourself. All you will need is both your eyes, your hands, and a rolled-up sheet of paper.

Keeping both eyes open, use your right hand to hold the roll of paper up to your right eye. Then, bring your left hand up to your left eye. The palm of your hand should be facing you and be about 6 inches (15 cm) away from your face. Make sure the little finger on your left hand is touching the paper roll. Now, when you look at your left hand with both eyes, it should look like part of your hand has become invisible.

Because you have the tube over one eye, your brain combines the right eye's view through the tube with the left eye's view of your hand. This results in the illusion that part of your hand is missing!

THE ROCHESTER LENS CLOAK

What if it was possible to make a cloak that would let you see through a person as if part of them was missing? Well, the Rochester Cloak uses a bunch of different lenses to do just that. Lenses are used to make this cloak because they are able to bend the light that travels through them.

A convex lens directs light inwards. The point where the light rays meet is called the focal point. The distance between the lens and the focal point is called the focal length.

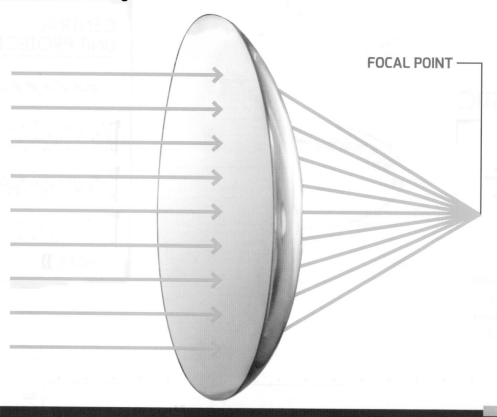

FOCAL POINT

THE BEST THING ABOUT THIS CLOAK IS THAT – UNLIKE THE OTHER ATTEMPTS AT INVISIBILITY CLOAKS – THE VIEWER CAN LOOK AT IT FROM MANY DIFFERENT ANGLES AND THE OBJECT WILL STILL APPEAR INVISIBLE.

The Rochester Cloak uses four different lenses to guide light rays around an object. If light rays don't hit an object, it means that we can't see it. As you can see, the cloaking region is widest between the first and second lens and the third and fourth lens, meaning that objects placed in these regions can become completely invisible! This is because light is being bent around these regions.

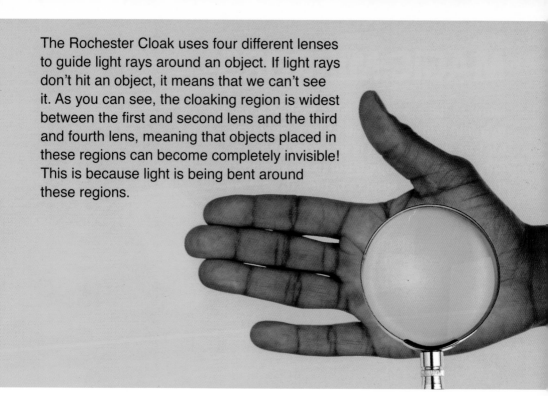

LIGHT RAYS

CLOAKING REGION

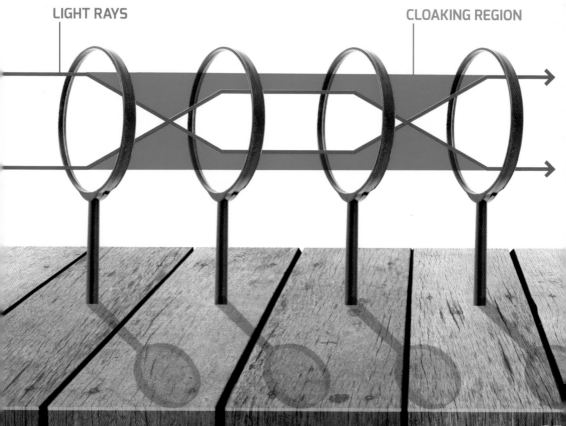

MAGIC MIRRORS

Many of the cloaks we have looked at try to guide light around an object. However, for true invisibility, it is important not only to hide an object, but to make sure that we can see what is behind it, as if we were looking straight through it. Mirror cloaks do this very well and, as a result, are popular with magicians who use them to make people "disappear."

MIRROR CLOAKS ARE A GREAT WAY OF HIDING OBJECTS AND EVEN PEOPLE, BUT THEY ARE QUITE BIG AND HARD TO SET UP. SO, UNLIKE THE WIZARD BOY'S LIGHTWEIGHT CLOAK, YOU WON'T BE ABLE TO CARRY THIS ONE IN YOUR BACKPACK.

HOW IT WORKS:

For disappearing tricks, two objects are normally used. One object will be part of the background and another object will be cloaked by the mirrors. The first object is placed in front of the farthest mirror (mirror one), which is facing away from the viewer. Thanks to the position of the mirrors, the image of the first object bounces from mirror one, to mirror two, to mirror three, to mirror four and finally into the viewer's eyes.

Due to the angle of the fourth mirror, the viewer cannot see their own reflection. Now, if something fell from the sky and landed in the cloaked region, the viewer would be able to see it falling until it fell behind mirror 4. At this point the falling object would disappear, but everything else would seem normal. The viewer would still be able to see the object in the background as if nothing had fallen in front of it!

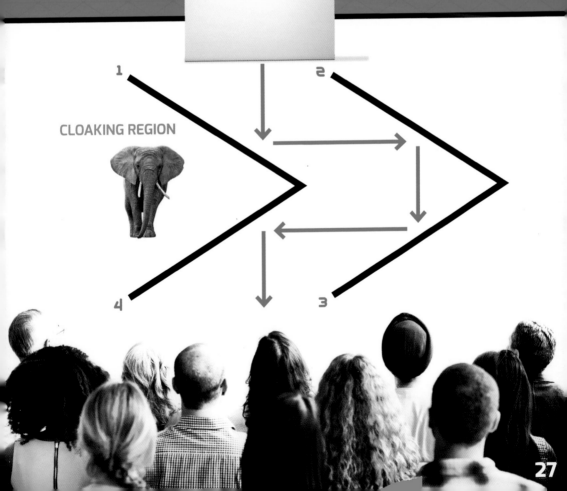

CLOAKING REGION

1

2

4

3

INVISIBILITY CLOAKS: THE FUTURE

CRIMINAL CLOAKS

So, you've heard the science fiction and the science fact, but are you truly prepared for a future where everybody, from dangerous criminals to your own grandma, owns an invisibility cloak?

People could get away with the most awful crimes and mischievous misdeeds if they knew they wouldn't be seen. After all, invisible criminals are much harder to catch! Sounds like a pretty terrifying future, right?

SPY GADGETS

But it's not all bad news. If you've ever dreamed of becoming a secret agent and taking down a supervillain or two, then invisibility cloaks could be your greatest tool in the fight against crime. With the ability to take criminals by surprise and spy on top-secret dealings, the secret agents of the world would be more powerful than ever before!

This might keep us all safe and sound, but it would hardly be fair if only the world's best agents got to own invisibility cloaks, would it? In fact, it's possible that invisibility cloak technology would be so useful to the world's most powerful organizations, that its discovery would remain a secret! Who knows? Perhaps they're already using them!

WHAT DO YOU THINK?

Invisibility cloaks certainly have their pros and cons, and that's without even mentioning the likelihood of bumping into invisible objects or misplacing your cloak! How would you find something you can't even see?

But, all things considered, it's up to you to decide. Invisibility cloaks – are they a dangerous weapon, or the latest, must-have spy gadget? Will you be saving up to have the latest cloak in your closet, or would you prefer to know what's around the next corner?

GLOSSARY

active camouflage	camouflage that changes and adapts to different backgrounds
carbon	a natural element found in materials like diamond and coal
convex	having an outline or surface which is curved outwards
electromagnetic spectrum	the range of waves created by association of electric and magnetic forces
engineered	designed and built
illusion	a deceptive appearance or impression
legendary	famous or relating to traditional stories
lenses	curved pieces of glass that can direct or disperse light
manipulate	control or alter
mantle	an old word for a cloak worn over clothes
microscopic	something that is so small that it can only be viewed by using a microscope
military	a country's army and things that relate to it
nanometers	units of measurement used to measure light
oasis	a place in the desert where water is found
philosopher	a person who studies the nature of knowledge, reality, and existence
predators	animals that hunt other animals for food
prey	animals that are hunted by other animals for food
spectrum	a scale, often with extremes at each end
surgeons	doctors who perform operations that involve cutting into someone's body to repair damage
transparent	a material that lets light pass through it, causing it to be see-through
trilogy	a collection of three books
urban	relating to a town or city

INDEX